African Wild Dogs

Victoria Blakemore

For Sir and his wild dog, with love

vblakemore.author@gmail.com

Copyright info/picture credits

Cover, Rich Carey/Shutterstock; Page 3, Mathias Appel/flickr; Page 5, skivvy/Pixabay; Page 7, Helen/AdobeStock; Page 9, Maciej Czekajewski/Adobestock; Pages 10-11, Iuliia Sokolovska/AdobeStock; Page 13, Lori Labrecque/AdobeStock; Page 15, Guy Bryant/AdobeStock; Page 17, Heather/AdobeStock; Page 19, WiseTraveller/Pixabay; Page 21, Seymour/AdobeStock; Page 23; Jez Bennett/Shutterstock; Page 25, Pexels/Pixabay; Page 27, Pexels/Pixabay; Page 29, Mathias Appel/flickr; Page 31, Mathias Appel/flickr; Page 33, Rich Carey/Shutterstock

Table of Contents

What are African Wild Dogs?   2

Size   4

Physical Characteristics   6

Habitat   8

Range   10

Diet   12

Communication   16

Movement   18

Pack Life   20

Pups   22

Wild Dogs and Humans   24

Population   26

African Wild Dogs in Danger   28

Helping African Wild Dogs   30

Glossary   34

What Are African Wild Dogs?

African wild dogs are medium-sized mammals. They are related to other canines, such as wolves, coyotes, jackals, foxes, and dogs.

African wild dogs are sometimes called painted dogs, hunting dogs, or painted wolves.

African wild dogs are a mix of
many colors. They can be black,
gray, brown, tan, gold, white,
and red in color.

Size

African wild dogs are usually between 2.5 and 3.5 feet long. Adults stand at least two feet high at the shoulder.

When fully grown, they usually weigh between forty and seventy pounds.

Male African wild dogs are a little bit larger than females.

Physical Characteristics

African wild dogs have large, rounded ears. They are able to move their ears in different directions. This allows them to hear prey from far away.

They only have four toes on their paws. This is different from other kinds of dogs that have five toes.

African wild dogs each have a **unique** fur pattern. No two wild dogs look the same.

Habitat

African wild dogs are usually found in grassy savannas. They sometimes travel to deserts, grasslands, and more mountainous areas.

It is usually very hot and dry where African wild dogs live. They have to get a lot of their water from the food they eat.

Range

African wild dogs are only found in Africa. They used to be found in about forty countries.

Now they are found in about twenty-five. Many are found in Botswana and Zimbabwe.

Diet

African wild dogs are **carnivores**. This means that they eat only meat.

Their diet is made up of large animals such as antelope, warthogs, and wildebeest. They also eat rodents, lizards, and birds.

When African wild dogs hunt

large animals, they usually chase

one that is sick or hurt.

When hunting, African wild dogs work as a team to catch their prey. They chase their prey from many sides to make it easier to catch.

They have a lot of **stamina** and can chase their prey for miles. This allows them to catch most of what they chase.

When they catch their prey,

African wild dogs share their

food with each other.

Communication

African wild dogs use sound, scent, and movement to communicate. They make sounds such as growls, whines, coos, and barks.

The adults mark their **territory** with their scent. This tells other wild dogs that the area is taken.

African wild dogs use

movements to show **affection**,

ask for food, and play with

each other.

Movement

African wild dogs have long, strong legs. They are able to run about thirty miles per hour for several miles.

Although they are better at running long distances, they can also run fast for short distances. They can run over forty miles per hour in a **sprint**.

African wild dogs are most active at dawn and dusk, when it is cooler. They have also been seen hunting at night.

Pack Life

African wild dogs live in groups that are called packs. A pack usually has around ten wild dogs.

Packs are lead by one male and female wild dog. They are in charge of the pack and choose where the pack hunts and sleeps.

Packs travel, hunt, and sleep together. They are very playful and may play-fight or wrestle.

Pups

African wild dogs usually have a litter of about ten pups. When they are first born, they are blind.

Pups stay in a den with their mother for several months. Other pack members bring food for them and their mother to eat.

Pups are taken care of by the rest of the pack. Most pups leave to start their own pack when they are about one year old.

Wild Dogs and Humans

People have tried to

domesticate African wild dogs.

They wanted the dogs to be

pets or help with hunting and

protection.

African wild dogs cannot be

domesticated. They do not trust

humans and **rely** on their pack

too much to live without them.

African wild dogs are just that,

wild. They are meant to live in

the wild, not with humans.

Population

African wild dogs are **endangered**. There are not many left in the wild. They could become **extinct** if their population continues to **decline**.

There are thought to be fewer than 6,000 African wild dogs left in the wild.

African wild dogs often live up to ten years in the wild. They can live longer in **captivity**.

African wild dogs are facing several threats. The main threat is habitat loss. Their habitats are getting much smaller and more spread out.

They are also hunted by humans in areas where people keep **livestock**.

African wild dogs are also

threatened by diseases like

rabies and distemper.

Helping African Wild Dogs

One way that people are helping animals like African wild dogs is by creating special **preserves**. They provide animals with safe habitats.

Wildlife **corridors** provide African wild dogs with safe ways to get from one protected habitat to another.

Some groups are working with **livestock** herders. They help them to make **enclosures** to keep their livestock safe from African wild dogs.

Other groups track and study wild dogs. They hope that knowing more about wild dogs will allow them to help keep them from becoming **extinct**.

Glossary

Affection: a friendly feeling, love

Captivity: animals that are kept by
humans, not in the wild

Carnivore: an animal that eats only meat

Corridor: a passageway or hall

Decline: to get smaller

Domesticate: to tame

Enclosure: an area that is surrounded by
walls or a fence

Endangered: at risk of becoming extinct

Extinct: when there are no more of an
animal left in the wild

Livestock: animals such as cows or sheep that are kept be people

Preserves: areas of land set up to protect plants and animals

Rely: to depend on

Sprint: running at top speed

Stamina: the strength to keep going for long periods of time

Territory: an area of land that an animal claims as its own

Unique: different, special

About the Author

Victoria Blakemore is a first grade

teacher in Southwest Florida with a

passion for reading.

You can visit her at

www.elementaryexplorers.com

Also in This Series

Gray Wolves — Victoria Blakemore
Sloths — Victoria Blakemore
Flamingos — Victoria Blakemore
Camels — Victoria Blakemore
Koalas — Victoria Blakemore
Honey Bees — Victoria Blakemore
Pandas — Victoria Blakemore

Pangolins — Victoria Blakemore
White-Tailed Deer — Victoria Blakemore
Orcas — Victoria Blakemore
Giraffes — Victoria Blakemore
Corn — Victoria Blakemore
Meerkats — Victoria Blakemore
Echidnas — Victoria Blakemore

Walruses — Victoria Blakemore
Raccoons — Victoria Blakemore
Bald Eagles — Victoria Blakemore
Apples — Victoria Blakemore
Arctic Foxes — Victoria Blakemore
Red Pandas — Victoria Blakemore
Cassowaries — Victoria Blakemore

Tigers — Victoria Blakemore
Ladybugs — Victoria Blakemore
Moose — Victoria Blakemore
Beluga Whales — Victoria Blakemore
Leopards — Victoria Blakemore
Elephants — Victoria Blakemore
Jellyfish — Victoria Blakemore

Binturongs — Victoria Blakemore
Lions — Victoria Blakemore
Dolphins — Victoria Blakemore
Reindeer — Victoria Blakemore
Hammerhead Sharks — Victoria Blakemore
Hippos — Victoria Blakemore
Pumpkins — Victoria Blakemore

Peafowl — Victoria Blakemore
Chameleons — Victoria Blakemore
Florida Panthers — Victoria Blakemore
Aye-Ayes — Victoria Blakemore
Black Bears — Victoria Blakemore
Cheetahs — Victoria Blakemore
Manatees — Victoria Blakemore

Gingerbread — Victoria Blakemore

Polar Bears — Victoria Blakemore

Hot Chocolate — Victoria Blakemore
Orangutans — Victoria Blakemore

Coyotes — Victoria Blakemore

Marshmallows — Victoria Blakemore

Strawberries — Victoria Blakemore

Also in This Series